INDIE AUTHOR MAGAZINE

HELLO AND WELCOME!

I'm Indie Annie, and I'm thrilled you're reading this gorgeous full-color version of IAM. Did you know that you can also access all the information, education, and inspiration in our app? It's available on both the iOS App Store and Google Play. And for those that prefer to listen to me read articles, you can pop over to Spotify or our website. Happy Reading!

X

IndieAuthorMagazine.com

DISTRIBUTION

PUBLISHER
Chelle Honiker

CREATIVE DIRECTOR
Alice Briggs

EDITOR IN CHIEF
Nicole Schroeder

COPY EDITOR
Lisa Thompson

WRITERS
Angela Archer
Elaine Bateman
Patricia Carr
Laurel Decher
Fatima Fayez
Gill Fernley
Greg Fishbone
Remy Flagg
Chrishaun Keller-Hanna
Jac Harmon

WRITERS
Marion Hermannsen
Kasia Lasinska
Bre Lockhart
Anne Lown
Sìne Màiri MacDougall
Merri Maywether
Lasairiona McMaster
Susan Odev
Nicole Schroeder
Emilia Zeeland

PUBLISHER
Athenia Creative
6820 Apus Dr.
Sparks, NV, 89436 USA
775.298.1925

ISSN 2768-7880 (online)–ISSN 2768-7872 (print)

From the Publisher

That dog won't hunt.

When I moved to Texas from California what feels like a million years ago, it sometimes felt as if I'd moved to a far more exotic locale than just a new state in the same country.

The food was different.

The BBQ meat looked burnt and inedible but tasted delicious, and everything was always covered in a thick american cheese sauce they called "queso" or in a gloppy white sausage gravy. I learned you could deep fry anything if you tried hard enough, including a twenty-four-pound turkey.

North, South, East, and West are meaningless.

I now needed to parse "thisaway" and "thataway" and discern how long "a spell" was when I asked for directions. I was once told, "Y'all go thisaway for a spell, and then turn thataway when you see the tree with the yellow ribbon tied to it." Not only did I never find that tree, I abandoned my trip entirely when I encountered a hissing armadillo in the middle of the road that refused to move.

And then there are the colloquialisms.

The first time I met my new in-laws, Uncle Joe-Boy said to my then husband, "She's got some snap in her garters." I wasn't sure if I should be offended, but I rightly took it to mean I was a sassy one. Over the years I had to dig out my Texas-English dictionary when he said about his sister, "She's two sandwiches short of a picnic basket," commented about any politician, "He's slicker than boiled snot," or when he angered a waitress and said, "She's in a horn-tossing mood."

As authors, we're able to imbibe our characters with a little color. We can let their personalities shine through descriptions and colloquialisms. As a reader, I love these little analogies. But much like my early Texas life, don't assume your reader will know what in the "Holy Sam Hill" you're talking about. Be sure the phrase stands on its own for readers from all countries so you don't pull them out of the story or send them running to Google something.

Otherwise, that dog won't hunt.

To Your Success,
Chelle
Publisher
Indie Author Magazine

PLANNING TRAVEL TO A CONFERENCE?

Use miles.

PLAN YOUR BOOKS
THE WAY YOU THINK

Outline faster, plot smarter, and turbocharge your productivity today with the #1 visual book planning software for writers.

USE CODE "IAM" FOR 10% OFF

https://writelink.to/plottr

Take Your Backlist to the Bank

Every single one of your old books is new to someone.

We struggle and fight endlessly to add readers to our newsletter lists. Beyond current and future titles, there is substantial opportunity in delivering your old titles to new fans. Introduce them to your backlist incrementally. I use sales and promotions of the first in series. Maybe even make the first book free if there are enough books in the series to earn your money back from the cost of the free promotion. It's okay to pay for someone to see your work. Fans have value that is worth your paying to find them.

A great book put into the right readers' hands. Those are the two concepts that every professional author must execute.

A great book? That may not be your first book, or your fifth, but it might be your sixth. It might be your twentieth too. How do you get better if you don't practice with intentionality? I write short stories to sharpen my craft. I've written a lot of short stories. And then I offer them for free to get new readers onto my list. If they like those stories, they look for other stories.

Backlist riches.

Simple as that. You can always sell a good book. Even if it's not great, readers are forgiving (not those one-star, bitter people, but they don't matter as much as you think). And the readers understand that this was a book written in the before time.

They expect you to get better as an author, but they also expect you might not have always written as well as you do now. If your first story is that bad, fix it. It's oftentimes easier to fix a story than write new words. When you're more experienced, dive in, and you'll find that with a few days' work, you'll be able to sharpen an old story, take it from good to great.

And you'll probably find that it wasn't as bad as you might have thought. Find the gems within your prose. Your readers have. And introduce those words to your new readership.

Because your words have value, and your backlist is a bank that you can always draw from. ◼

Craig Martelle

Craig Martelle

High school Valedictorian enlists in the Marine Corps under a guaranteed tank contract. An inauspicious start that was quickly superseded by excelling in language study. Contract waived, a year at the Defense Language Institute to learn Russian and off to keep my ears on the big red machine during the Soviet years. Back to DLI for advanced Russian after reenlisting. Deploying. Then getting selected to get a commission. Earned a four-year degree in two years by majoring in Russian Language. It was a cop out, but I wanted to get back to the fleet. One summa cum laude graduation later, that's where I found myself. My first gig as a second lieutenant was on a general staff. I did well enough that I stayed at that level or higher for the rest of my career, while getting some choice side gigs – UAE, Bahrain, Korea, Russia, and Ukraine.

Major Martelle. I retired from the Marines after a couple years at the embassy in Moscow working arms control issues. The locals called me The German, because of my accent in Russian. That worked for me. It kept me off the radar. Just until it didn't. Expelled after two years for activities inconsistent with my diplomatic status, I went to Ukraine. Can't let twenty years of Russian language go to waste. More arms control. More diplomatic stuff. Then 9/11 and off to war. That was enough deployment for me. Then came retirement.

Department of Homeland Security was a phenomenally miserable gig. I quit that job quickly enough and went to law school. A second summa cum laude later and I was working for a high-end consulting firm performing business diagnostics, business law, and leadership coaching. More deployments. For the money they paid me, I was good with that. Just until I wasn't. Then I started writing. You'll find Easter eggs from my career hidden within all my books. Enjoy the stories.

Dear Indie Annie,

I'm working on a series of nonfiction books that I hope will help people with issues they may struggle with. I'm not a professional in my field; I've just learned a lot through life experience. Can I write from my own experience? Or do I need a degree or certification to help people?

School of Hard Knocks in Sussex

DEAR SWEET, HUMBLE HARD KNOCKS,

What do you think I'm going to tell you?

Many could challenge me on what qualifications I have to provide the carefully crafted, loving advice I give in this column every month. And if they even had the cajones to question this to my face, what would my answer be?

I am Indie Annie, the guru of indie writing. I bring enlightenment. I bring wisdom. Who grants me the authority to make such claims?

I do.

I look back over my life in indie publishing and pronounce (eloquently, of course) that I have knowledge and experience that can help you in your career.

Do I know everything? No, I don't.

Do I have a PhD in indie publishing? No, because no one does. There's no such thing.

I *might* have a degree in creative writing, graphic design, or rocket science. Equally, I might not have a certificate in anything other than the one-hundred-yard breaststroke I got when I was seven.

But I have lived my life and learned many valuable things along the way. And now, I choose to spend some of my valuable time crafting answers to my readers' wonderful questions. Is that wrong?

I think not.

Did the great sages of the past have college certificates? What qualified Aristotle to write about philosophy or even writing, for that matter, except that he was a revered expert in one and a student of the other? I mean, arguably, Aristotle spent twenty years as a pupil

and colleague at the Academy of Plato (c. 428–c.348 BCE), but did he have framed copies of his qualifications nailed to the wall of his office in the Lyceum?

Though I can't prove it, I am pretty sure the answer to this is no.

My point is, who defines what you have to say as being of value? Your audience.

Do you think there is an audience for your nonfiction books? Do you think you have sufficient insight into a subject that, once published, would benefit another? If the answer is yes to both questions, then you have a duty to write what you have learned and share your wisdom with the world.

My darling Hard Knocks, you do not state what field you would write in, but let's ponder a few options. Have you learned how to manage an addiction? You may not be a qualified counselor, but your story would most definitely help others traveling the path you once trod. Perhaps you are a business owner who can guide budding entrepreneurs through the stages required to build a successful enterprise, though you never set a foot in Harvard Business School. Maybe you are a self-taught musician who has developed a unique system for learning new instruments, and you are planning to write a series of beginner's guides to the flute, lute, and harpsichord.

Only you know if you can help someone else with your books. Are you able to solve a problem they face? If the answer is yes, then write away, my dear friend.

I suspect your fear lies less in the writing of your series and more in its promotion. How will you market a series when you appear to have no credentials? Why would anyone buy from you? Are you some quack selling snake oil?

Well, like the snake-oil sellers of old, it's all about the pitch. People don't buy credentials; people buy hope. They buy answers, so if you are solving a problem, you are more than halfway there. And they buy into the person who is selling. Make sure your blurb sells *you* and announces clearly that *you* are what they have been looking for.

Do you have a guaranteed way to lose weight, make a killing in Vegas, or sell a thousand books? Can you organize the cluttered? Motivate the listless? Or teach a starving college student how to boil an egg?

I leave you with the works of one Mrs. Isabella Mary Beeton (1836–1865). Her legendary guide to Victorian housekeeping is one of the best-selling books of all time. And what were her qualifications? She was a young Victorian housewife, nothing more. But it was more than enough.

Happy writing,
Indie Annie

10 TIPS FOR
PATREON

Patreon, an online platform, allows people to financially support creatives, including authors, through a monthly tiered membership. It offers an excellent option for any indie author looking to diversify their income and create a new revenue stream.

But how do you optimize your profile on the platform for maximum returns on your time investment so that you entice existing fans as well as new readers and supplement your income at the same time? Read on for our top ten tips for mastering Patreon.

1 MAKE THE MOST OF THAT FIRST IMPRESSION

A profile on Patreon without an introduction will quickly turn away potential patrons. Introduce yourself, your books, and your genre. Welcome visitors to your page, and let them know what you'll be offering should they become your patrons. In turn, share what their support means to you and what they're helping you achieve through their pledges. You can even remind your current fans just why they clicked through and became a patron.

Bonus points if you include a welcome video—people often appreciate putting a face and a voice to a name. A video is much more personal than a block of text. Through the video, you'll also show visitors that you're active on the platform, serious about it, and that ultimately, it's a great idea for them to become your patron. In that vein, you could also create a personalized thank-you video for those who do click through and become patrons. This will make them feel special and connected to you.

Also, don't assume that everyone visiting your Patreon page will know who you are. Make sure to include a link to your website or Amazon author profile to help convert random browsers into patrons.

2. LIST A RANGE OF TIERS

You'll want to give your potential patrons a variety of options to choose from. That way, they can adjust their pledges accordingly. A one-dollar tier is a great entry point for patrons who wish to support you but who may not be able to afford more expensive tiers. Nonfiction author Joanna Penn offers the benefits of a simple thank-you and a hug if you ever meet the patron in person. Other benefits of higher tiers include listing the patron on her website, access to a bonus monthly Q&A, and polls on character or setting names. You could even offer patrons special roles on your private Discord server.

Likewise, an exclusive, extravagant, or expensive tier for superfans could also be an excellent idea if it fits in with your business model. Mountaindale Press publisher and author Dakota Krout has a one-thousand-dollar tier, in which he promises to fly the patron to anywhere in the continental United States, buy them dinner, and hand deliver a signed copy of all his books and a clothing item. For a superfan, that would be a dream come true.

3. BRAND YOUR PATREON

Treat Patreon as part of your business, and make sure that it aligns with your website and other social media platforms in terms of look and feel. Give your tiers names related to your books, and include header photos that relate to your books and your brand. This will create a cohesive experience between all your platforms and will make your patrons feel as if they're part of your world.

4. GO BEHIND THE SCENES

You may wish to offer behind-the-scenes glimpses into your process as one of the benefits of joining a particular tier. These could include your outlines, handwritten notes, edits, or deleted scenes. These are invaluable to readers, who often want to see your creative process and glimpse "how the sausage gets made."

5. DON'T OVEREXTEND YOURSELF

This is an important one: Don't try to do too much. It's easy to get carried away and fill your tiers with all sorts of goodies for your patrons—after all, they're handing over their hard-earned cash to support you, so you want to keep them happy. But left unchecked, Patreon can become a full-time job and eat into your writing and production time.

It's better to offer items that you already produce as part of your process. (See tip 4.) These can include bonus or deleted scenes, early access (which requires no new content), or polls for cover art or character names. You can even offer to list your patrons in the acknowledgment section of your next book—this takes minimal effort on your part, but readers will be thrilled to see their names in a published book. You could also list their names on a dedicated part of your website with an optional link back to their own website or social media profile.

6 CONSIDER "CHARGE UP FRONT"

If you're publishing content regularly on your Patreon (for instance, chapters of your books as you write them, or early e-book copies of your books), then you may wish to consider the "charge up front" option. If you select this option, your patrons are charged both when they join and again on the first of the month as opposed to only being billed on the next first of the month. For instance, if a patron joins on July 20, they will be charged on July 20, then again on August 1, only twelve days later. You could add a disclaimer to your profile, clarifying the policy and advising potential patrons that if it's close to the end of the month, they might wish to wait until the first of the next month. That way, they won't be charged twice in a short time frame.

The upside to the "charge up front" option is that you won't get a patron who checks out your content, downloads your patron-only e-book, and cancels their pledge before the first of the month without paying anything. The downside is that potential patrons won't be able to see what's behind the paywall and decide if they like your content enough to become a regular paying patron.

Pro Tip: Author beware—once you change to the "charge up front" option, you can't change back to the default billing method. So choose wisely.

7 SET GOALS

You may also wish to set goals on your Patreon. Goals are a great way to track your progress on the platform and to let your patrons know where the funds you raise will go. For instance, you could set goals for audiobook production, new covers, editing—the sky's the limit.

In addition, goals involve your patrons in your creative process. They can follow along and help you reach that next milestone in your career.

8 HAVE SOCIAL PROOF

When you're just starting out on Patreon, you may want to ask a friend or relative to contribute at a lower tier.

By default, anyone who visits your Patreon profile can see both how many patrons you have and the total amount that you make per month. You can hide one (or both), but it may be a smart idea to keep the number of patrons visible. This could encourage potential backers to support you, especially when they see they won't be the only one.

This is why it's extremely important to get those first few backers on board—social proof works wonders when it comes to convincing those who may be on the fence.

9 OFFER MERCH

Everyone loves physical rewards. They're tangible and often make recipients feel like their pledge was money well spent.

Patreon now offers merchandise fulfillment on its website for a range of items: clothing (T-shirts and hoodies, among others), tote bags, prints, stickers, mugs, or posters. Simply customize the item and choose a tier, and Patreon will handle fulfillment, tracking, delivery, and support.

By wearing or exhibiting your merch, patrons are also supporting you and your brand externally. That's a win-win for both of you.

10 BE CONSISTENT

Consistency is king. Your patrons are contributing to your business financially every month, so be sure to put out new content at least once per month. You don't want your patrons—who are arguably your most loyal supporters—to feel shortchanged.

Posting new content more than once a month is often better, but remember tip 5: Don't overcommit. Patreon should be a natural extension of your business, not an all-consuming, full-time job. It is, however, a versatile platform, and you can certainly tailor it to fit you and your business' needs. So go out there, create your tiers, and have fun! ■

Kasia Lasinska

How Nick Thacker Is Rewriting the Rule-book

THE THRILLER WRITER SAYS TRADITIONAL PUBLISHING IS BROKEN. HE'S GOT PLANS TO FIX IT.

When someone called Nick Thacker's novels "airplane books" early on in his career, he took the term and ran with it. The description was meant to be an insult—as in his books were the kind you buy at an airport to help kill time during your flight. But to the Action-Adventure Thriller author, the comment was high praise. If you can pick up one of his novels and be entertained for a few hours, Thacker says he's done his job.

"I'm not trying to win a literary prize," he says. "I don't want to win the Pulitzer. My prose isn't artistic. I'm treating this like what it is, which is entertainment. And I want to do that well."

Many would likely say he's succeeded in that respect. After ten years in the industry, Thacker has published around thirty books, and by 2017, he was making enough money to turn his author business into a full-time career. Along the way, he's also undertaken projects that boost independent authors around him, including a radio station for writers (https://radiowrite.com) and an email marketing service (https://authoremail.com). Six months ago, he embarked on his newest venture: launching Conundrum Publishing, a traditional publishing company that seeks to right the wrongs of other traditional publishers.

"What he's doing with Conundrum Publishing is revolutionary," writes Kevin Tumlinson, an author, podcaster, and the director of marketing and public relations at Draft2Digital—as well as a close friend of Thacker's. "He's taking the best strengths of both indie publishing and traditional publishing, throwing out the bits that don't work, and building a platform that can nurture authors and books in a

specific genre. ... And it's a replicable system he can apply to more genres, going forward. He's building an empire there."

WORK-LIFE-WRITING BALANCE

You'd think Thacker would've always enjoyed writing with the way his life looks now. But when he was still in school, the future author hated it. He swore he'd never write long-form again if he could help it.

Then, in 2011, his grandfather died. In the wake of his passing, Thacker decided to write a book to gift to his father, just like the Thriller paperbacks the three would often swap. After all, he asked himself, how hard could it be?

"I knew nothing at all about anything," he says. Convinced he would only write one book, he tried to fit every trope and idea he could think of into a single story. It didn't work. Some time and a few books on craft later, he had a finished manuscript—plus a list of ideas he'd had to cut out that would work themselves into his later novels—and began querying agents for a traditional publishing deal. He didn't even know Kindle existed at the time, but when he discovered Kindle Direct Publishing (KDP), he decided to give it a try.

He didn't find instant success with the first book, but the process sparked something in Thacker; he kept writing. "I guess I enjoyed it more than I thought I did," he says. Even while juggling a job at his church and raising two kids, he would find time "in the cracks" to jot down new books a few sentences at a time.

By early 2017, he'd started to make money for a few bills each month, and his wife suggested he focus his energy on either his author career or day job instead of stealing time from both. After a few months, he made his decision official—he quit his job to pursue writing full time. Anxiety set in a day later. "All the sudden, I was faced with, 'Wow, if I don't show up and do the job every day, then we don't get to eat next month,'" he says.

The pressure of that transition to full-time was challenging, Thacker says. He'd come to the publishing world with a minor in entrepreneurship and marketing, but textbooks hadn't quite conveyed the realities of the business model. The stress weighed on him; for a time, Thacker struggled with panic attacks and severe anxiety. "I definitely still struggle with it," Thacker says. "If I'm left to my own devices and let my guard down, I will start to feel anxious." But he's also learned to manage it over the years and embrace his diagnosis—something he encourages others to do as well.

"Let's make this part of the discussion of what it means to be a full-time author because there's some version of this that we're all struggling and dealing with," he says.

BREAKING TRADITION

As Thacker has spent more time in the industry, his interests have broadened beyond just writing books. He's become involved in the indie author community, speaking at conferences and sharing advice and tools with newer writers. He uses his marketing background to manage Author. Email, a publishing-focused email marketing service. He offered an author coaching service for a time—it was how he met Tumlinson in 2013. Now the two joke that Tumlinson bought him as a friend during that session. "He owes me two hundred bucks," Tumlinson says.

Along the way, he also received advice from other authors he met, with one message in particular cropping up regularly: that an author could generally find more success through self-publishing than traditional publishing. Thacker agreed, but he wanted to prove himself right. So he sought a traditional publishing deal of his own.

Thacker's Jake Parker series was published with Bookouture in 2020, and he says they are some of the best books he's written. And though he emphasizes that the publishers at Bookouture were fantastic, "as an industry, traditional publishing is, in fact, broken," Thacker says. Among its faults, traditional publishers are stuck in a business model that favors selling print books over competing with Amazon and independent authors, he says. "They're just a little bit antiquated." As for the Jake Parker books, Thacker urges anyone interested in reading them to wait a few years—he's hoping to republish the trilogy once his seven-year contract is up.

But for every problem traditional publishers carry, Thacker believes self-published authors have the solution. His answer comes in the form of a new traditional publishing company. Conundrum Publishing models a different approach to the publishing process, Thacker says. Where most traditional companies hire developmental editors, Conundrum brings manuscripts in front of "the roundtable," a team of four or five professional authors in the same genre who can critique the books from a market perspective. Where other companies use human copy editors, Conundrum reduces cost by running books through a machine learning tool known as the AI Gauntlet. The books are then distributed to a two-hundred-person street team of beta readers and ARC readers. The company pays for advertising once the book is released and gets paid a percentage of royalties—it only succeeds if the author does, at no upfront cost to the latter. "I always tell people, at Conundrum Publishing, our MO is 'authors win first,'" Thacker says.

Conundrum was born out of the publishing company Thacker started when he began publishing books, but it only officially launched earlier this year. Already, the company has signed between fifteen and twenty authors and is set to have published fifty books by the end of 2022. "There is so much that we could do as an industry that isn't being done yet. We're on the cusp," Thacker says. "My goal is to be a part of that."

THE NEXT ADVENTURE

When he looks to the future, Thacker has goals for every part of his career. He wants to grow his author business and continue writing, and he wants to help Conundrum grow as well. The publishing company exclusively publishes Thrillers at the moment, but he hopes it will one day expand to include other genres.

He has ideas for the future of the self-publishing industry too—a distinction he doesn't always believe will be necessary. "We're going to call it publishing in the future [instead of self-publishing]," he says, referencing a phrase he'd heard from Tumlinson. He believes independent authors are on the verge of gaining more recognition and a louder voice in the book publishing world.

When talking about another close friend, author Ernest Dempsey, Thacker shares nothing but praise for his dedication to writing and his work's caliber. "He's the pinnacle—the consummate professional, if you will. I'm always getting distracted by other crap," Thacker says. But those side projects reflect Thacker's dedication to helping other indie authors. And for every challenge and distraction that comes with author life, Thacker also sees reward in a simple fact: he likes to make stuff up for a living. "To be able to put all these things together in a way that I think is entertaining and that I think makes sense—it's exactly the kind of stuff that I would've wanted to do as a kid if I had known that that's what writing was," he says. He hopes other authors at any stage in their writing careers can realize the same.

"I often get lost in the details. I often get stressed about how much stuff I have to do. And the best thing I can do for myself is remind myself that I'm a writer," he says. "Writers write. Don't lose sight of the core thing, the core activity, we do." ■

Nicole Schroeder

Mining for Gold

STRIKE IT RICH WITH BOOKS ALREADY ON YOUR AUTHOR SHELF

If you have published multiple books, then you may be working with two "lists." Your frontlist is made up of newly published, fresh, exciting titles. Your backlist is books that have been out for a while that might be neglected by you and by readers. But gold is buried in the backlist, and you owe it to yourself and your readers to mine that gold for all it's worth.

Many of the best methods for increasing backlist sales are similar to, if not the same as, what you would do for a new release, but these titles offer some interesting possibilities you'll want to explore. We list them in order of least to most difficult to do; though none are hard, some may just take longer than others.

OTHER BOOKS BY ...

As you're releasing a new book, consider adding an "other books by ..." page in the back of the book after your "about the author" page. A linked list in your e-book makes it very easy for readers to click over and keep on reading. New readers who loved the book they just finished reading will be excited to read even more from you, and longtime readers who might've missed a couple of your earlier releases will be thrilled to discover these lost-to-them titles.

The downside to having a comprehensive list in the back of the book is that you need to update this list every time you publish another book. In the beginning, when you have only a few titles out, this is fun and exciting. But it can get tedious quickly. And if you publish frequently and use IngramSpark, it can get expensive as well, even with free codes for some updates.

Pro Tip: Link to a page on your website that you can easily keep updated with links to all your books instead of updating each book individually. Or link to the series page on Amazon if you're exclusive with them. These evergreen links will not need updating.

Consider using the cover image and blurb as an advertisement in the back of your book. Many traditional publishers do this not just for the author of the book but for their other authors as well. You could promote the first in a series of a related series or a title in the same or a similar genre that might catch the eye of the reader and draw them to more of your books.

Pro Tip: Images can increase deliverability costs for e-books, so use a small file size to keep these costs low. Six hundred to eight hundred pixels wide is usually sufficient, though you may want it smaller for a longer blurb.

PROMOS AND STACKS

As with a new release, you can periodically promote your backlist titles in the same way that you would a new release. Frequently, this is done with the first in a series. Newsletter swaps, ad blasts, and other promotional sites can inject some life into your sales.

Price promotions are also effective, <u>according to BookBub</u> (https://insights.bookbub.com). Many of the most successful indie authors offer the first book in a series as permafree. If you're not a fan of making a book free for all time, discount it for a limited time to create a bit of a buying frenzy.

Backlist titles are great for group promotions and book bundles as well, writes author Daniel Parsons in <u>a blog post for Self Publishing Formula</u> (https://selfpublishingformula.com). Gather a group of authors in your genre, and create a book bundle of the first book in each of their series. Cross promotion will help all of you attract new readers and give you a great excuse to make a lot of noise on social media. Then, watch the gold roll in.

RELAUNCHING

If your book has been out for a few years, you might want to critically look at its cover. Cover design trends change. This is more of an issue for fiction than nonfiction titles, as nonfiction cover trends have a longer lifespan than do many fiction genres. Still, you may not have nailed the cover the first time around, or perhaps it could use a refresh. If so, a new look is a solid excuse for relaunching your book with all the fanfare of a new title. You might be surprised at how much an on-trend cover will increase your profit margins, even with the extra expense of the cover.

NEW EDITIONS

Are your books in all the available formats? If you originally published an e-book only, a print version will add to your repertoire, and you can tell your fans about it. If you have print, think about creating some additional content and doing a special-edition hardcover version. Professionals at Reedsy <u>suggest including additional features</u>, such as a map, character artwork, additional illustrations, or a Q&A with you or your characters. Audio is a growing format that is worth considering as well.

Pro Tip: Commissioning maps and illustrations can be expensive, so consider other ways to use those assets as well, such as in merchandise, social media posts, or special rewards for contest winners.

If your original version didn't include them, discussion or reflection questions can provide additional engagement for readers. These questions can work just as well for fiction as they do for nonfiction, and they'll make your book a strong contender for a book club.

BOOK SETS

If your series has reached a decent length, combining the first three or more books into a book set can be another format that you can promote and use to gather fresh eyes. Often these are also called box sets, but unless you actually put them in a box, it's best to avoid using that specific term.

If you have several related series, you can also put the first one or two books from each into a book set to introduce readers to all of your series.

Book sets can be short or long, so combining smaller sets into a series omnibus can also effectively attract more readers.

GOING WIDE

If your books have always been in Kindle Unlimited, you might find a larger readership on other platforms than just Amazon. This will be genre dependent. Some authors have found greater success outside of KU than in. Your mileage may vary, so do some research first on what successful authors in your genre are doing, and recognize that it takes a while to build readership, so you may not find instant success. Wide readers are not the same as KU, so be willing to experiment with promotions and ads to find the right mix.

TIME- OR TOPIC-SENSITIVE TITLES

If your book is set during a holiday season, B&H Publishing Group (https://bhpublishinggroup.com) recommends promoting it during that season every year to gain new readers. You might think about creating a holiday-themed book set if you have several that you could include. What about a "Through the Year" set if you have several books set in different seasons or holidays?

Keep an eye on the news and trending topics on social media. If you have a book that would address or relate to that topic, then seize the opportunity and promote it quickly and widely. If you can enter the conversation people are already having in their heads or with others, then you'll be hitting a very effective target.

BUT WAIT, THERE'S MORE ...

We don't have time or space for additional ideas here, but this list should help spark your creativity and give you new tools to mine your backlist's gold.

- Remind readers of backlist titles with social media posts, as Craig Martelle of 20BooksTo50K® suggests in his Successful Indie Author Five-Minute Focus series
- Use an older title as a reader magnet
- Create a spoiler alert Q&A for your blog, YouTube, or newsletter
- Design merch
- Remind your readers to review your books
- Post a book quote on a great graphic on social media, as MK Williams, of Author Your Ambition (https://1mkwilliams.com), explains
- Offer review copies
- Participate in library or bookstore readings and signings, recommends author and editor Chrys Fey in an article for Fiction University (http://blog.janicehardy.com) ∎

Alice Briggs

AUTHOR·TECH·SUMMIT

Begins: August 30, 2022

AuthorTechSummit.com

Need tech to increase your productivity and profits?

Join us for free, and get to know the tools and classes that will help you keep cool in the current economic weather conditions.

Have a tool or class? Let's chat.

11 Ways to Earn More from Your Nonfiction

You've no doubt heard the truism, "Don't put all your eggs in one basket." But if you're a nonfiction author still selling on only one platform, your income eggs are tightly packed into one container.

You can make money in a myriad of ways from your nonfiction backlist. Create multiple streams of income for yourself, and no matter what might happen to your platform down the road, you won't run the risk of being left hanging.

That's easy to write, but where do you begin?

To start, you need passive income as well as active income.

When you write a freelance article or provide consulting, you have to do the work every time you want to make money, and you can only sell that article or consulting time once. That's active income. And given we have only twenty-four hours in each day, you might really struggle to scale your income past a certain point if that's all you do.

However, when you create an asset, such as a course, video, or book, you can sell that product thousands of times without ever creating anything else. That's passive income. Of course, you still have to do some work to sell what you've created—passive income isn't completely passive. But you're not exchanging time for money anymore. There's really no limit on what you can earn with that model.

You've already worked toward having passive income if you have a nonfiction backlist. Here are just some ways you can bring in new income streams to ensure you thrive in your nonfiction career:

1) CROSS-PROMOTE YOUR BOOKS

The easiest way to make more money from your nonfiction is to add links in the back of each of your nonfiction books to promote the rest of your backlist.

Nothing is stopping you from referencing and recommending other books you've written within the content of your other books. Don't overdo it, though. A common complaint in reviews for some nonfiction books is that the author appears to be simply copying from and promoting their other books in the text rather than writing anything new.

As long as you know what you've linked to is genuinely helpful, this technique should work for you.

2) MAXIMIZE YOUR FORMATS

E-book, print, large print, hardback, audiobook. How many of those different formats have you set up? You've already written the content. All you need to do is change the format of your current work, and you'll have a whole new product. You'll also be catering to people who prefer to listen rather than read and to people with disabilities.

3) TRANSLATE YOUR BOOKS

English is an international language, but there's a whole world out there. At the time of this article, Amazon alone will let you self-publish in over forty different languages, and they're working on adding to that.

Why not take advantage of that and break into global markets?

4) ADD WORKBOOKS

People love to work through exercises and guided prompts when they're learning something new. Could any of your current books benefit from accompanying workbooks?

If you create a workbook for each nonfiction title you already have, you've just doubled your published books and created another product for people to buy.

5) CREATE COURSES

How many e-books do you need to sell to bring in a thousand dollars compared with a single thousand-dollar course? We'll let you do the math. You can create a large course based on your whole book, a series of minicourses based on each chapter, or both, as long as each course offers solid value to your readers. Add video and audio, checklists, worksheets, planners, and anything else that might be beneficial. You could even offer a small email course delivered automatically by an autoresponder.

Don't forget to encourage people to join your email list with a lead magnet, such as a bonus e-book or free course. Once they're on your list, you can market your newest nonfiction books, courses, and any other products.

6) SET UP A MEMBERSHIP

Recurring monthly income, for the win! Package your knowledge into a continuing membership where people pay a fixed fee every month to learn from you.

If you charge only ten dollars a month but have anywhere from a few hundred to a thousand members, your income will see a nice boost.

7) OFFER COACHING AND CONSULTING

The more access people have to you, the more they will pay if they want to learn from you. You could charge a higher rate for group coaching than you would for a course, and an even higher rate for one-to-one coaching—all from the knowledge you already have.

8) RECOMMEND OTHER PRODUCTS AND COURSES

If you sign up as an affiliate for other businesses, you will earn a commission if someone buys their product through your affiliate link. The best type of affiliate income is recurring income where you are paid every month to sell a product once.

You can add affiliate links to your courses, blog posts, your email signature, your website copy, your email newsletters, and more. Find affiliate products and courses to promote that relate to the subject matter covered in your nonfiction. Just note, the Federal Trade Commission requires that you state that these links are affiliate links.

Do your research and only recommend relevant products that you really believe in. Your reputation matters, and you don't want to damage it by recommending unethical or unhelpful products.

9) GET YOUR MERCH ON

Think beyond books to merchandising opportunities. You could sell mugs, T-shirts, key chains, bookmarks, tote bags, note-books, stickers, and more, all branded to fit with your books and your author business. You can do this directly on your website, on Etsy, or via a site such as Zazzle (https://zazzle.com) or RedBubble (https://redbubble.com).

10) SPEAK AND EARN

You can be paid to speak at conferences and events. If you're comfortable with this, it can be an excellent stream of income and a great opportunity to promote your nonfiction books. In addition to payment for speaking, you can also receive travel expenses and accommodations, depending on the event.

To find speaking opportunities, get to know other speakers and conference and event organizers. Join related Face-book groups and look out for author events, literary festivals, and other suitable events. Network to find out about opportunities, and be proactive in approaching organizers.

Pro Tip: Don't forget to bring physical copies of your books so that you can sell them at the event after your speech.

11) SELL THE SHOVEL

Who got rich in the gold rush? The people who sold the shovels.

If you're a highly successful nonfiction author, can you teach others how to publish their own nonfiction work? You might have your own specialist subjects for your books, but if you've done it for long enough, you'll know a whole lot about writing nonfiction and making a success of it.

Your knowledge is valuable, and people will pay for it. Consider doing the following:

- creating a series of small courses on different aspects, such as research or planning.
- writing a nonfiction book on how to write a nonfiction book (very meta!) or on self-publishing.
- setting up a membership for people who want to learn from you.
- providing group coaching.

These are only some ways to make more money from your nonfiction books. You could also consider sites such as Patreon or Kickstarter, sponsorships, licensing your content, private label rights, and more.

Take it slow! If you try to do everything at once, you'll find yourself stuck or burned out very quickly. Add one stream of income at a time and build it up little by little when you know you have the time and the mental space for more. Eventually, you should see your income increase over time, and you'll find that you're no longer reliant on just one income stream or platform.

One final bit of advice: Don't limit yourself. Keep thinking about what you can adapt, and keep an eye on technology. New possibilities are emerging all the time. The current craze for NFTs has hit the publishing world, for example, and you could find a way to get your own slice of that pie. Who knows what might be invented next?

The only certainty is that there is no certainty. If you have multiple streams of income, you're more likely to be protected from the vagaries of the publishing world and the global economy.

And that creates real peace of mind. ∎

Gill Fernley

ScribeCount Wants to Be Your New Best Friend

TIME IS MONEY, AND THE SALES DATA TOOL AIMS TO SAVE YOU BOTH

ScribeCount bills itself as an indie author's best friend—and if you're looking for a platform that provides deep insight into your aggregate sales data, then its claim may be true. With the ability to collect data from multiple sales platforms, customize your own reports, and a pricing structure that flexes with your monthly sales, ScribeCount has the potential to become a valuable addition to your indie author toolbox.

The folks behind ScribeCount, Randall Wood and Phillipa Werner, are authors themselves and set out to create a product that would become the preeminent author service platform on the internet. A quick glance at the program's testimonial reel shows that they've won over more than a few bestselling authors, so it may be well worth your time to spend a few minutes checking out what ScribeCount has to offer.

HOW DOES IT WORK?

The ScribeCount browser extension allows you to gather your sales data from multiple platforms and display them in a single reporting session. It currently supports the following sales platforms and plans to add more in the near future:

- Amazon
- Google Play
- Apple
- Barnes & Noble
- Kobo
- Draft2Digital
- Smashwords
- IngramSpark (coming soon)
- Audible (coming soon)
- Findaway Voices (coming soon)

The extension is optimized for use with most common browsers, such as Google Chrome, Microsoft Edge, and Firefox. The website lists Safari as an option that will be coming soon. The processing and storage of your data is done in the cloud and protected with the same type of encryption used to protect government data. An in-depth technical explanation of <u>ScribeCount's Privacy Policy regarding your personal data</u>, storage, and encryption capabilities can be found on its website.

Once you've installed the ScribeCount extension to your browser, all you need to do is open the extension, log in to ScribeCount, and visit each of your sales pages to establish the connection between ScribeCount and the sales page.

Once you initiate a reporting session, ScribeCount pulls the following data elements from your sales pages every fifteen minutes and displays them in a convenient and customizable dashboard format:

- sales numbers
- ENP data
- book IDs
- book ranks
- book reviews
- book prices
- KU enrollment dates
- geographical sales data, both current and historical

https://www.kboards.com/threads/scribecount-now-with-a-ku-dashboard.335556/
Retrieved 6/9/2022

The ScribeCount dashboard contains a combination of interactive charts and graphs that let you slice and dice your report data as needed. This is great for tracking sales promo results, ad performance, read-through rates, and more.

Subscribers can remove their data from ScribeCount's servers at any time by doing one of the following as stated in the program's FAQs:

- "Disable all the connections to the platforms and then log out. If you [choose] this option, ScribeCount stops asking for data, your doorman shuts the door, your settings are deleted, and your data is purged from our servers. Logging out in this fashion means the purged data will need to be reloaded to start another session, requiring a longer wait time."
- "Keep connections enabled and use the 'Delete my Data' button to purge your data without losing your settings."

If you're a strictly KU author, don't feel left out. ScribeCount's custom KU dashboard works just as well for you as it does for wide or hybrid authors.

WHAT FEATURES ARE AVAILABLE?

The extension was built with Bootstrap open source, which means it will work just as well on your table or mobile devices as it does on your computer. The extension is designed to run only while your session is active, which means it will not run in the background and chew up your processing capacity or battery life.

Authors who have both wide and KU sales data have the option to switch between separate dashboards for each sales channel.

One of the nicer features this product offers is full access to the product's functionality for every subscriber, regardless of the pricing tier. This is quite the deviation from most of its competitors. The ScribeCount site lists the following report-focused features available to all subscribers:

- customized dashboards to fit the wide or KU author
- dynamic reporting from all the major platforms

- a worldwide sales map showing the countries where your books are selling
- a news feed that is updated regularly, keeping you informed of what's happening in the world of indie publishing
- downloadable spreadsheets in Excel format so you can easily customize your income and expenditures
- current and historical data updated every fifteen minutes

ScribeCount plans to add more sales and advertising platforms each month and to expand its product offerings to include production, marketing, and translation tools.

Additional features include

- the ability to choose from three different KU Page Read rates
- the ability to manually add KU Bonuses to earnings reports
- the ability to choose your preferred time zone and currency display
- twenty-four-hour customer service (phone, chat, and email)
- an affiliate program that pays you 10 percent of each person's tier amount for those who sign up through your link
- access to the ScribeCount blog, which features articles, advice, and platform information of interest to indie authors
- the ability to filter or drill down into specific markets, pen names, titles, and more via the dashboard

HOW MUCH DOES IT COST?

Pricing is based on your monthly sales income and will adjust based on your earnings. As with any other business-related subscription, ScribeCount is tax deductible, and the company provides subscribers with a yearly payment report.

ScribeCount currently offers a fourteen-day free subscription, no credit card needed, after which the following pricing tiers are available:

- Tier 1: $0/month for authors earning less than $1000/month
- Tier 2: $15/month for authors earning between $1001 and $2000/month
- Tier 3: $20/month for authors earning $2001 or more
- $185 Flat Rate Yearly Subscription

At the end of the 14-day free trial, subscribers are sent a sign-up form and asked to choose a payment method. ScribeCount currently accepts the following payment methods:

- PayPal
- Via Stripe:

    - Visa
    - MasterCard
    - American Express
    - ACH (direct debit from your bank account)

Once you've entered your payment method, ScribeCount will verify your previous month's sale income and charge your preferred payment method for the appropriate service tier. Similar to KU's payment structure, your sales total for the previous month will determine your pricing tier for two months forward. For example, your sales total in June 2022 will determine the amount you're billed August 1.

Subscribers are free to cancel at any time by clicking the Cancel My Subscription button. Cancellations will be processed within forty-eight hours, and any charges made in error will be refunded.

Considering everything that the platform currently offers and the company's focus on continued development, ScribeCount seems to be an affordable, robust, user-friendly service that would make a powerful addition to any indie author's toolbox. ∎

Jenn Mitchell

Tech Tools

Courtesy of IndieAuthorTools.com
Got a tool you love and want to share with us?
Submit a tool at IndieAuthorTools.com

Books2Read Universal Links

Simplify the management of your link library with Books2Read Universal Links.

You can customize your universal link to focus on a specific storefront or book format. When Draft2Digital first introduced the free author service, the links were only available for digital books. Now you can use the simple, evergreen links across other book formats from audiobooks to print to hardcovers.

https://books2read.com/

Author Unleashed Face-book Group

In this Face-book group, members "explore the cutting edge of book marketing as detailed in the Author Unleashed series by Robert J. Ryan." Discussion topics range from running profitable Amazon ads to writing professional-level copy for blurbs.

https://www.face-book.com/groups/1056593901397144

UptimeRobot

Track your author website's uptime with this online monitoring service. On the free plan, you can monitor up to 50 URLs at 5-minute intervals. The app is available for iOS and Android. If your business plan includes direct sales of books or merchandise, downtime detection could be a valuable tool.

https://uptimerobot.com/

Evernote

Ranked as one of the best apps for taking notes, Evernote auto-syncs across your devices, enabling you to invite anyone to collaborate on any project. This versatile app lets you save and organize text, videos, photos, and audio recordings.

https://evernote.com/

Pozotron Studio

Quickly proof your audiobooks with Pozotron. This AI-powered software suite lets you cut hours from the audiobook production process. Its accuracy-checking algorithm takes care of catching word mismatches, so your mind is freed up to focus on the creative elements like tone, performance, and character consistency.

https://www.pozotron.com/

TRIGGERED

INDIE AUTHORS WEIGH IN ON THE CONTENT WARNING DEBATE

Author Mariel Pomeroy left a cautionary message for readers of her debut novel that is hard to miss. It's printed on its own page in the front of the book just after the copyright. She also included it in the book's product description and in her social media posts advertising the novel. A general statement about the genre is even in the bio of her Instagram account.

Almost everywhere readers might find her book, she made sure they could also find trigger warnings for its content.

"It wasn't even a question if I was going to put it into my book or not," says Pomeroy of Book Daddy, LLC. "I would rather you look at my book, you read the trigger warnings, or even the genre—I ended up a couple of weeks ago putting 'This is a Dark Romance High Fantasy' before the summary on Amazon—so you know exactly what you're walking into."

· CAUTION · CAUTION · CAUTION · CAUTION ·

In recent years, the use of trigger warnings online and on social media has grown considerably, according to *The New Yorker* (https://newyorker.com), raising the question for authors and their publishers as to whether they should follow suit. But so has the controversy surrounding the warnings. Some, such as Pomeroy, consider it an important step in allowing readers to make informed decisions about what they read, but others argue it is unnecessary, citing genre expectations, a reluctance to generalize audiences, and concerns of censorship.

The debate has expanded beyond the reader community. Professors have fueled the fire by providing trigger warnings for some classic books and well-known authors, according to the United Kingdom's *The Week* (https://theweek.co.uk). Critics of the practice, including the National Council of Teachers of English (https://ncte.org/statement/rating-books/), have likened it to the book-banning trend that experienced a resurgence in the past year when more than one thousand titles were banned in United States school districts between July 2021 and March 2022, according to Education Week (https://edweek.org). Scientific studies have also called the practice into question with results that suggest trigger warnings offer little to no benefit to survivors of post-traumatic stress disorder (PTSD). The term "trigger" is technically a psychology term used in reference to mental health conditions like PTSD.

Still, many readers emphasize how beneficial trigger warnings have been for their reading experience—and how harmful the lack of them can be. In the years since internet users began integrating trigger warnings into mainstream use, alerts to sensitive content have become almost expected in certain online communities, reports Buzzfeed News (https://.buzzfeednews.com)—and corners of BookTok and

Bookstagram are no exception. Pomeroy says part of the reason she was so intent on including warnings for her own work came from knowing people who have experienced traumatic responses from distressing themes in books. "I've seen a lot of people that I know personally have very strong reactions and truly see a trigger warning and be like, 'Oh my god, I cannot read this.'"

But for Sapphic Fiction author Adrian J. Smith, the question of whether to include trigger warnings doesn't have a clear answer. Smith considers herself a "reservist" when it comes to the warnings. Only one of her books has ever included a trigger warning, which came at the decision of her publisher for depictions of torture and sexual violence. And although she agrees with adding warnings for those types of subject matter, she believes many other commonly flagged themes are redundant when readers look at the genre or the book's blurb.

"If you write or read Dark Romance, putting a trigger warning for kidnapping is just stupid because it's expected in the genre. If you write Post-Apocalyptic fiction or even a lot of Urban Fantasy or Sci-Fi, putting a content warning for violence is kind of stupid because, again, it's expected," Smith says.

In a similar vein, Smith says triggers in the psychological sense are too varied and subjective to adequately label everything that may affect a reader. In the same book where her publisher flagged some of her content with trigger warnings, other potentially triggering themes from the novel were left alone that she thought might've deserved a warning, and reviewers pointed out still other taboo topics in the book.

Overall, Smith says she prefers the term "content warning" to "trigger warning" as it removes ties to medical diagnoses and therefore any assumptions about how your readers might react. Yet even this doesn't fix the challenge for those writing "on the edge of taboo" according to society's standards, such as those who include LGBTQ+ content, like she does.

"Ten or fifteen years ago, I would have needed a content warning for my book because my main character is a lesbian. And now in 2022, I don't need that, but you're also not likely to find my books in a high school library," she says. "A lot of people still put content warnings on BDSM books. I have written a couple, and I won't do that because BDSM is just a way of living. It's a way of loving a person differently than some other people do it. And it's not necessarily a bad thing. It's just content."

THE QUESTION FOR AUTHORS

So what options do authors have regarding how to write warnings in their own work?

In the self-publishing industry, a lot. Almost every decision rests on the author's shoulders, including whether to write a warning regarding a book's content in the first place. For those who still struggle with whether they should write a note, however, Pomeroy says she suggests asking alpha and beta readers their thoughts on the book's content and what they think might require a warning.

She says she believes any sort of regulation or standardization for the practice would be difficult, though she encourages authors to make their warnings as easily accessible as possible. List warnings in the product description, inside the front cover, and on your author website, she suggests. As for the wording of the note, there are ways to be thorough without revealing too much of the story. Pomeroy says she's planning on changing her method for the second book in her series in order to be more descriptive.

"What I've seen authors do and what I want to do going forward is do that [provide a list of general themes in the book] and then, especially for the e-book version, include

a link to my website for a literal list," she says. The URL would provide those who are unsure about the book's content with more context regarding sensitive scenes without the risk of spoiling major plot points for others.

"Everyone's lines are different," Pomeroy says. "So something that might not be a trigger for me might very well be a trigger for someone else."

Looking at the debate from another perspective, Smith says authors should consider their genre and audience as they write trigger warnings for their books. If readers can readily expect sensitive themes based on the genre or the cover blurb, she says, you might not need to be as descriptive in your note—if you need to include one at all.

Ultimately, as with any creative industry, there isn't a correct answer for how to handle sensitive content in books. When all is said and done, however, Pomeroy says she roots her decision more in her beliefs as an artist than in her strategy as a business owner.

"There's not a reason not to list trigger warnings," Pomeroy says. "I want the people who are going to genuinely enjoy the things of this and the genre of this to read it, completely independent of sales or numbers or anything like that. That was the point of this book in the first place. Of course, I want it to be a career. But numbers are probably the last thing on my mind when it comes to this, especially when it comes to sensitive topics." ▪

Nicole Schroeder

Pro Tip: Authors and readers can visit http://BookTriggerWarnings.com or http://TriggerWarningDatabase.com, online trigger warning databases, for lists of the types of content that might require a warning and to browse current entries or create new pages for books not yet included in the databases.

Podcasts We Love

The Paperback Podcast
https://podcasts.apple.com/us/podcast/the-paperback-podcast/
id1448015223

Business coach and host Pagan Malcolm says this weekly show is for ambitious and aspiring authors. She specializes in helping them "to understand the business side of publishing and create a lifestyle that supports [their] authorly goals." Recent topics have included marketing your backlist, preventing prelaunch mistakes, and maintaining momentum.

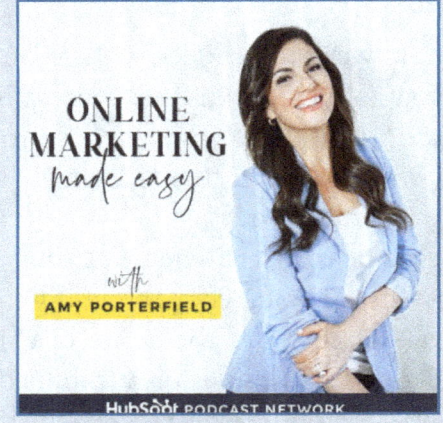

Online Marketing Made Easy with Amy Porterfield
https://podcasts.apple.com/us/podcast/
online-marketing-made-easy-with-amy-porterfield/id594703545

Need help converting big ideas and strategies into actionable, step-by-step processes? That's marketing strategist Amy Porterfield's specialty. While her top-ranked podcast isn't designed specifically for indies, you'll find valuable information about list building, marketing, and social media.

Unstoppable Authors
https://podcasts.apple.com/us/podcast/unstoppable-authors/id1403887471

Follow three indie authors on their adventures in self-publishing on Unstoppable Authors. Recent episodes covered creating multiple streams of income, planning and running an author event, and raising creative children. Join Holly Lyne, Julia Scott, and Angeline Trevena for more on the writing life on Mondays.

The Truth about Texas:

WHY THE LONE STAR STATE MIGHT BE THE PERFECT SETTING FOR YOUR NEXT BOOK

When you think of Texas, a few images might come to mind: cowboys, hot prairies with dusty tumbleweeds, herds of cattle, chuck wagons, horses everywhere, the Alamo, and more.

As with every American state, these are typical stereotypes with roots in reality. And sure, you'll find all those things in Texas in some form or fashion. But when authors write about Texas, they could use a lot of imagery beyond the typical.

MAIN CHARACTERS REJOICE: TEXAS HAS DIVERSE ECOREGIONS

Need to hide a body in a sand dune? There are 367 miles of shoreline facing the Gulf of Mexico with a chain of seven tropical barrier islands, stretching from Galveston Island to Brazos Island. Rather than

tumbleweeds, the lush coastline could be mistaken for any gulf coast town in Florida with plenty of seashells and sandy beaches. Just remember that the sun sets over land rather than sea, so plan your majestic sunset rendezvous accordingly.

Moody, gothic east Texas could be mistaken for Georgia or Louisiana with its moderate rainfall and lush rose gardens. Vampires and other supernaturals could blend in easily, inhabiting antebellum-style homes complete with moss-laden trees and plenty of bogs perfect for midnight roaming. Its piney woods could easily feel like home to a pack of werewolves.

Meet-cutes between rival winery owners need not be confined to California or France. Texas' Hill Country with its rolling hills, proximity to winding rivers, and ample sunshine has fast become a tourist destination for food and wine enthusiasts, often being compared with Napa Valley.

West Texas is often thought of as the Texas standard with flat, dusty plains and oil derricks dotting the landscape. It's dry and arid, but as the saying goes, "If you don't like the weather, give it a minute." It can go from sunny to snow in seconds.

The ecoregions of Texas offer new possibilities for settings, and these are just a few of the more obvious options designed to spark your imagination.

IT TAKES A WHILE TO GET FROM A TO B

Texas lives up to its reputation as a big state, and it might be easy to mistake how long a character realistically needs to get from one city to another. The following map will give you a better perspective.

If Texas were its own country, it would be the fortieth largest, and larger than every country in Europe, according to TexasProud.com.

The longest line from north to south through the state as the crow flies is 801 miles. That's nearly two hundred miles longer than the United Kingdom's longest straight line from Land's End in England to John O'Groats in Scotland. In fact, nearly three United Kingdoms would fit inside Texas. Moreover, ten countries—Belgium, Czech Republic, Switzerland, Austria, Slovakia, Slovenia, Macedonia, Luxembourg, Hungary, and the Netherlands—could fit inside Texas without overlapping.

Traveling anywhere in Texas takes time. If you're writing about getting around Texas, bear in mind no central transportation system or railway connects the state's major cities of Dallas/ Ft. Worth, Austin, San Antonio, or Houston. To get from A to B, one must drive, often on what are known as farm-to-market, or "FM," roads. These roads were designed for what their name implies—getting from rural farms and ranches to markets, meaning that it's not a straight shot between places once you're off the main highways.

Pro Tip: Use driving distance calculators to accurately describe the time it takes to travel within the state.

THINK OUTSIDE THE BIG BOX

The geographical diversity and sheer size of Texas could make it an interesting setting in an author's work if one looks beyond the typical. There's more than enough to work with to ensure you keep readers engaged—just be sure to get the details right. True Texans will notice if you don't—you can hang your cowboy hat on that. ■

Chelle Honiker

Tale as Old as Time, Retold

Remember those first stories we heard as children? "The Three Little Pigs," "Little Red Riding Hood," "Three Billy Goats Gruff," "Snow White," "Cinderella," and so many more? We could listen to them over and over again. Each time, we were delighted with the end. The main character defeated the villain, found true love, and—my favorite—lived happily ever after. These stories transcend time, extend to all cultures, and resonate with all generations.

We call them fairy tales.

They were meant to teach lessons and life skills while entertaining us, but they are more than that. As authors, we can use fairy tales as a foundation to recreate or retell stories. An entire genre has been constructed for this purpose.

In 2021, Midnight Voss' Romance Writers of America (RWA) workshop, "Reinventing Fiction: Adapting Fairy Tales and Public Domain Classics Into Original Fiction," offered authors advice on how to navigate the genre. Author Shonna Slayton (https://shonnaslayton.com) has also written several books and blog posts on the subject over the years. They are just a few of the great resources available for authors who are interested in these stories. But before we go diving into writing with fairy tales, an aspiring author should know some basics.

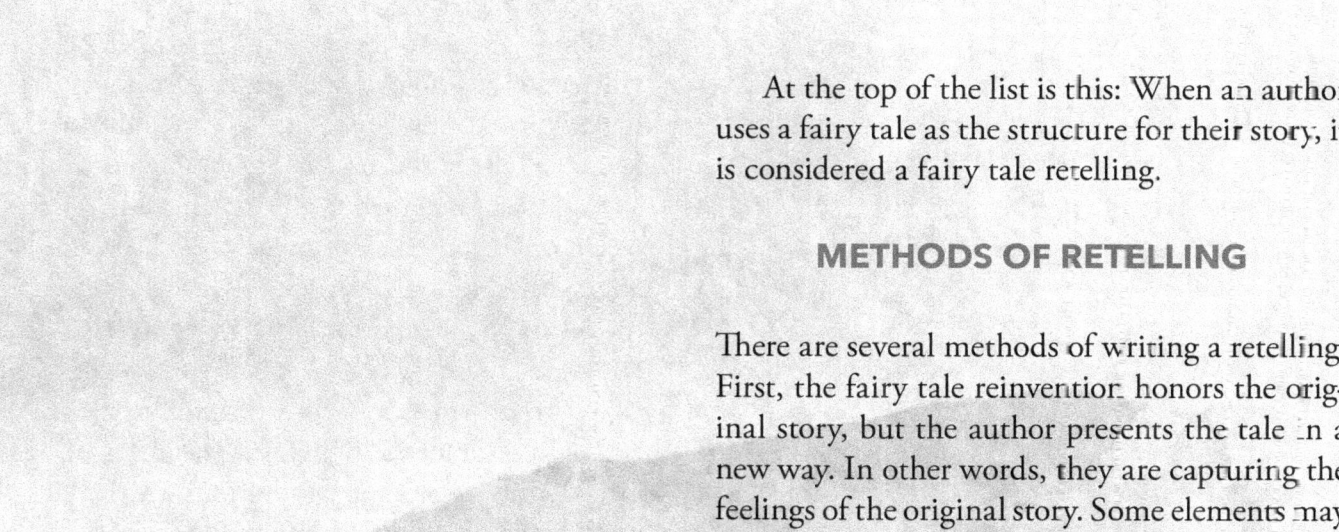

At the top of the list is this: When an author uses a fairy tale as the structure for their story, it is considered a fairy tale retelling.

METHODS OF RETELLING

There are several methods of writing a retelling. First, the fairy tale reinvention honors the original story, but the author presents the tale in a new way. In other words, they are capturing the feelings of the original story. Some elements may be changed, but otherwise, the author remains true to the story premise.

"Little Red Riding Hood" is a classic example. The original version of "Little Red Riding Hood" written by Charles Perrault was a cautionary tale of what could happen when a young woman divulges too much personal information to a stranger. Although the message is still relevant, the author may choose to present a different theme. In contemporary retellings, Red or the wolf are the main characters with a story arc showing the conflicts they bring to the story and how they grow through their obstacles.

Next, the recreation of a fairy tale tells the tale in a different setting. It will have the same outcome as well as several icons to connect the readers to the original story.

Lastly, the "kitchen sink" method of retelling brings several stories together. The characters interact with each other and add to the story arc. This method comes with a warning. Don't be fooled by the abundance of material. Of the methods for fairy tale retellings, the kitchen sink has the most demands. The magic systems or setting parameters within the different story worlds cannot compete with one another. Braiding plotlines in the kitchen sink method requires asking questions about the story concepts and planning on which elements will enrich the plot and which can fall to the wayside.

> When an author uses a fairy tale as the structure for their story, it is considered a fairy tale retelling.

Here are a couple of things to remember when retelling a fairy tale: Readers of this genre have expectations. Some parts of the adaptation need to reflect the original story. Think Snow White and the mirror, the seven helpers, the quest on behalf of the prince, and the awakening brought on by true love's kiss. This isn't meant to be a limitation; it is a way to have fun with the material.

With all three methods of retelling, setting is also a character. It dictates the rules of the story world, expressing limitations on the character as well as adding potential for outcomes.

Fairy tale retellings are fun for readers and writers alike because they touch on themes that elicit delight and the feeling of already knowing the story. However, the retelling is that much more fun because it combines the comfort of the familiar with the excitement of a new approach.

COMMON RETELLING TROPES

Bargain: The character makes a deal as a means of negotiation to save oneself or a family member

Betrayal: A person the character trusts tries to kill them

Evil Stepmother: Sometimes referred to as the bad parent trope, the new family member who brings unjust misery to the main character

Disguise: A side character pretends to be an ally, but their intent is to bring harm to the main character

Friends Are Family: The character fleeing their circumstances meets a band of friends that becomes their support system

Love Conquers All: True love's kiss will remove the curse, and the royal in search of love will find it with the main character of the story

Poverty: The character lives in circumstances where they are starving or lack finances, which drives them to seek assistance from someone with magical powers

Transformation: The character changes into their true self

Trials: The character must complete a task or otherwise reckon with severe consequences ■

Merri Maywether

The 'Eyes' Have It

STUDIES SHOW YOU DON'T NEED FANCY EYEWEAR TO PROTECT YOUR SIGHT FROM EXTENDED SCREEN USE

Blue light-filtering glasses sound like the perfect solution to computer eye strain. Unfortunately, there's no evidence to support their effectiveness. Systematic reviews of multiple studies, in 2017 and 2021, found no benefits to the lenses. Double-blind clinical trials found no difference between people wearing blue light-filtering glasses and those who weren't during tasks that varied from twenty minutes to two hours.

In 2022, the scientific journal *Sensors* published a report on a solution that relies on Fresnel lenses— the lenses used in lighthouses—"to avoid eye fatigue during long-term work close to the eyes." The Chinese and Ukrainian researchers even created a jazzy sample pair sporting the Ukrainian colors.

Basically, the new lenses make your eyes look at something near as if it were far away. When we work at the computer, we focus both our eyes on one point on the screen. Putting prisms in the lenses bends the light so it becomes parallel instead of hitting your eyes at an angle.

It's too early to know if prism glasses are the wave of the future. In the absence of a tech solution, what do we do to protect our eyes?

Eye professionals seem to agree on the basics:

1. **Keep your eyes hydrated** with eye drops if necessary. Keep yourself hydrated too. Surprisingly, coffee may help.
2. **Blink (see #1)** because screens make us forget. If you wear contact lenses, blinking is even more important. We're talking a lot of blinking. Participants in one research study blinked for ten seconds every twenty minutes for four weeks.
3. **Look into the distance.** Go outside and look at the horizon. Give your eyes variety. In one 2016 study, undergraduate nursing students reported less eye fatigue after eight weeks doing eight kinds of exercises: "palming, blinking, sideways viewing, front and sideways viewing, rotational viewing, up and down viewing, preliminary nose tip gazing, and near and distant viewing."
4. **Use glasses** with the right focal length for your task if you wear them. Your desktop, laptop, tablet, and phone are all at a different distance from your eyes.

Did you think to blink? Good for you! ◾

Laurel Decher

RESOURCES

Singh, S., Downie, L. E., & Anderson, A. J. (2021). Do Blue-blocking Lenses Reduce Eye Strain From Extended Screen Time? A Double-Masked Randomized Controlled Trial. *American Journal of Ophthalmology, 226*, 243–251. https://doi.org/10.1016/j.ajo.2021.02.010

Le, Zichun, Evhen Antonov, Qiang Mao, Viacheslav Petrov, Yuhui Wang, Wei Wang, Marina Shevkolenko, and Wen Dong. 2022. Anti-Fatigue Glasses Based on Microprisms for Preventing Eyestrain. *Sensors* 22, no. 5: 1933. https://doi.org/10.3390/s22051933

Kim S. D. (2016). Effects of yogic eye exercises on eye fatigue in undergraduate nursing students. *Journal of Physical Therapy Science, 28*(6), 1813–1815. https://doi.org/10.1589/jpts.28.1813

Cultural details are wrong.

How to Conquer the
Bad Review Blues

Too much Snow White, not enough Dwarves

Too dark. Gave me nightmares.

Lots of typos, I couldn't finish it.

The moment you've been dreading is finally here: your first bad review. You stare at it, wondering if you've misread it, then read it several more times. Each negative word feels like a tiny dagger to the heart. For some of us, there are tears. For others, there's cursing, hand-wringing, or an inner critic that mocks us. But the point is this—bad reviews hurt.

It's okay to take a few minutes and let it sting. You've poured yourself onto the page, and criticism is bound to cut you to the core, but do yourself a favor and don't let harsh words blind you to the fact that even the most scathing review can be turned into marketing gold. Plenty of savvy authors have done it, and you can too.

Sometimes we just have to chalk bad reviews up to the fact that you cannot please everyone. Understanding this is key when it comes to audience targeting. Take a deep dive to see what you can glean about the person from their review, then use it to refine your ad strategy.

Next, be honest with yourself. Is there some truth to the review that will help you improve your craft? My first bad review was titled, *Why Use 3 Words When 10 Will Do?* It temporarily crushed me, but the reviewer was spot on. My writing wasn't tight. Fixing that improved read-through, which translated to increased profit.

Lastly, try handling it like author and creator of the Self Publishing Formula, Mark Dawson. In 2019, he received a letter from a man who felt that his own writing was superior to Dawson's. He described Dawson as a talentless hack who wouldn't recognize skill if it "sucked" him in the face. Although harsh, the letter was hysterical. Dawson shared it and some passages from the other author's work with the Self Publishing Formula audience and during his 20Books Vegas keynote address later that year. The engagement was massive and even resulted in a spin-off line of revenue-generating merchandise featuring phrases from the letter and the other author's work.

So the next time you get a bad review, turn your frown upside down, and buck up, buttercup. You've just been handed the opportunity to turn a negative into a positive cash flow. ■

Jenn Mitchell

Plot is thinner than a bean pole, but a fun story.

5 Tips for Adding Diversity to Your Draft—and Doing It Right

Writing about topics that do not belong to your culture can be tricky. In today's society, writers venturing into those areas are sometimes worried about being accused of cultural appropriation, or the use of topics from other cultures for gain or profit or in a way that reinforces stereotypes. Even more so, we're taught as authors to "write what you know," and crafting a story involving another culture can be daunting if you know little about it. The problem is that in today's world, we crave diversity, especially in our entertainment. Our books are no exception.

So how does one write about a culture they are not familiar with?

Bringing other cultures into media is not a new concept. It's been done for thousands of years. In 2002, the West was introduced to Japanese lore in the form of movies. *The Ring*, *Shutter*, *The Grudge*, and more were adapted for the United States. These Japanese movies deserved to be seen all over the world, but in American culture, where audiences still struggle with the idea of reading subtitles, filmmakers cast Caucasian actors in the roles, allegedly to make them more appealing to American viewers. What isn't widely known is that the directors of the original Japanese films were often involved behind the scenes—*Ringu* writer Hiroshi Takahashi worked on *The Ring*, uncredited, and helped write its sequel, and Ju-On director Takashi Shimizu directed its American counterpart, *The Grudge*, according to IMDb. This allowed the adaptations to retain the essence of the legends. For instance, *The Ring (Ringu)* was based on Okiku's ghost, Japanese lore from the sixteenth century, and relocating the tale to America helped millions of people learn about it for the first time.

Before that, across four decades, Sidney Sheldon often wrote books set in faraway countries, ones we could only imagine. In 1974, Dean Koontz released the ever popular *The Key to Midnight*, which largely took place in Japan. Caucasian American author T. C. Boyle produced the incredible book *The Tortilla Curtain* in 1995, which introduced many to the struggles of immigrants. *Memoirs of a Geisha*, a highly celebrated book and movie, was originally released in 1997 and penned by a Caucasian American male, Arthur Goldman.

There is great precedent for positively writing about cultures other than your own; however, there are also examples of when that goes terribly wrong. The movie *The Curse of La Llarona* cast a Caucasian woman in the leading role against a backdrop of Mexican actors. Backlash swiftly ensued when the film was released. *Ghost in the Shell* is an extremely popular Japanese manga, but when reproduced in the West as a live-action film, Scarlett Johansson was the lead actress instead of a talented Japanese actress.

Writers and screenwriters fear the label of appropriation—with good reason—due to movies like this. In *Quartz* in 2015, lifestyle reporter Jenni Avins wrote, "As we watch artists and celebrities being pilloried and called racist, it's hard not to fear the reach of the cultural-appropriation police" (https://qz.com/520363/borrowing-from-other-cultures-is-not-inherently-racist/). Today, we are cautioned about not writing about other cultures, and entire groups on Face-book are dedicated to ripping apart anyone who dares write outside their race, ethnicity, gender, or culture.

But it has been done—and done successfully—so do not let that fear resonate in you. It is not necessary to deprive oneself of a valuable study into something with which you are not accustomed in order to provide an insight into that culture for readers. Time and again, you can see excellent examples of how to bring other cultures into your work. But a fine line exists between doing so positively and appropriation. So we now return to our original question: How does one write about a culture they are not familiar with? Here are five points to remember:

1. RESPECT

Nothing is worse than writing about another culture because that area of the world is now "popular" or "sells well." When you write for profit only, your book will suffer many downfalls, including being disrespectful to the culture on which

you are earning money. Respect is the number one point to remember when writing outside your own walls. You are a writer dipping your pen into others' lives, traumas, and history. You are in their world; they are not in yours. Traversing with the utmost respect is always required, even after the book is published and marketing begins.

2. AVOID

It's all too easy to fall into the trappings of stereotypes. We see them so much in entertainment that it's hard to differentiate what might be cultural and what is a stereotype forced on that culture. This makes the next point oh-so-valuable.

3. RESEARCH

As writers, if we don't know something, we research it—and hopefully not on Wikipedia. When you are writing about another culture, though, you need to take your research to the next level. Ensure you are gaining knowledge through reputable sites, preferably ones from that region. Reading books or watching movies from that culture is highly beneficial. With the internet, you can easily find people from that area who can tell you what's what and can read your story before publishing to make sure your content is right. In cases where you are writing LGBTQIA+ or disabled characters, you can also locate sensitivity readers or those within the communities for accuracy.

4. DISCOVER

If your story is fluid and can exist in any culture, such as a horror writer seeking a lesser-known legend or curse, open yourself up to the world. Many peoples are highly underrepresented, even in today's diverse society. OzMari Granlund, author of Dark Fantasy based on Filipino lore, wishes more authors would explore her culture as it is often overlooked in favor of more well-known areas, like Japan, China, and South Korea. "Our monsters and concept of fear is vastly different from the West," she says. "The Philippines alone have over three hundred eighty types of fantastical creatures that the West has never even heard of." The Aswang Project is a wonderful website that can take you down that tunnel of all those creatures. Sites like these are filled with ideas for new stories and topics that Westerners have never heard of or conceived.

5. RECOGNIZE

Recognize the value that other cultures bring to the world. This goes right along with respecting traditions and history. We have such a vibrant world filled with so many tales, and they are rarely found in your backyard. Remember and recognize what a culture has been through historically and

how they may have been misrepresented in the past and commit yourself to doing it right through research.

One might think that just because their skin is white and the other culture has white skin, they can write those characters without concern. But it's important to note that many of those, whether Caucasian, Black, Hispanic, Native American, or Asian, have differences in their legends, lores, and history that do not belong to others with the same skin tone. Don't limit yourself to only certain areas of the world. Award-winning author Jalpa Williby often visits other cultures in her work, and that includes disabled characters, such as in her book, *My Perfect Imperfections*, in which the lead character has cerebral palsy. She says, "Individuals with disabilities are significantly underrepresented in mainstream media. How many heroes are in wheelchairs?"

Writing about other cultures can be fun, provide wisdom, and give you a newfound respect for people all over the world. Now that you have the knowledge to move forward on a multicultural journey, only one question remains: Which one will you discover first? ◾

Argie Martin

From the Stacks

Courtesy of IndieAuthorTools.com
Got a book you love and want to share with us?
Submit a book at IndieAuthorTools.com

Relaunch Your Novel
https://www.amazon.com/dp/B071HVZD1G
Audiobook available

Learn how to implement a relaunch strategy to revive sales of your backlist books in Chris Fox's *Relaunch Your Novel*. He also covers how to establish an automated system that funnels readers through your catalog of books. This guide is part of the Write Faster, Write Smarter series.

Author Unleashed: Advanced Publishing and Marketing Strategies for Indie Authors
https://www.amazon.com/dp/B07YQDKZ4S/

Have you ever wondered why a great book sinks into oblivion while an ordinary book sells? Robert J. Ryan answers that and many other book marketing questions in *Author Unleashed: Advanced Publishing and Marketing Strategies for Indie Authors*. This book is filled with practical advice written in an engaging, easy-to-understand style.

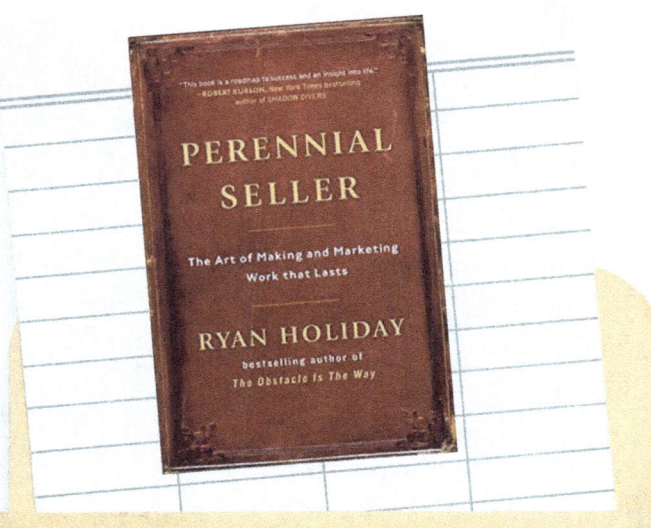

Perennial Seller: The Art of Making and Marketing Work that Lasts
https://www.amazon.com/dp/B01N8SL7FH/
Audiobook available

In *Perennial Seller*, best-selling author and media strategist Ryan Holiday explores what it takes to create a timeless piece of work – one that sells year after year. He shows you how to position and market your book as well as how to build a platform to ensure ongoing success.

This Is Marketing: You Can't Be Seen Until You Learn to See
https://www.amazon.com/This-Marketing-Cant-Until-Learn/
Audiobook available

To paraphrase iconic marketer Seth Godin, marketing isn't just selling books. To him, the core of the process is communication and connection, not the selling of things to people. *This Is Marketing* is the distillation of the insights he's gleaned from decades of experience.

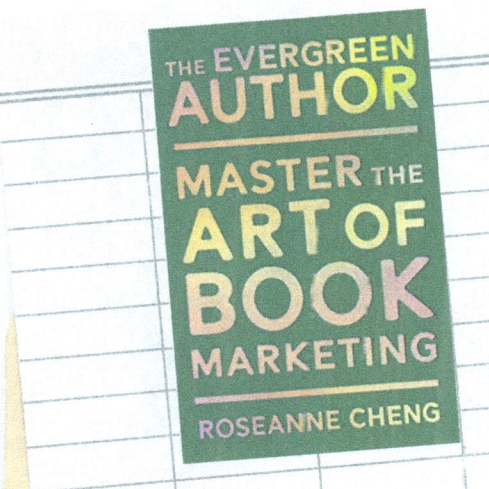

The Evergreen Author: Master the Art of Book Marketing
https://www.amazon.com/Evergreen-Author-Master-Book-Marketing-e-book/dp/B08NHKVBV3/?tag=indieauthortools-20

Audiobook available

The *Evergreen Author* provides a step-by-step system for successfully publishing your work and growing your readership. Its practical, actionable advice will help "to keep you accountable and on track from pre-launch, to launch, and beyond."

LastPass ®

KEEP YOUR PASSWORD SAFE

Auto-pilot for all your passwords

Writelink.to/lastpass

Design like a Pro for free

 Try Canva Pro today

https://writelink.to/canva

In This Issue

Executive Team

Chelle Honiker, Publisher

As the publisher of Indie Author Magazine, Chelle Honiker brings nearly three decades of startup, technology, training, and executive leadership experience to the role. She's a serial entrepreneur, founding and selling multiple successful companies including a training development company, travel agency, website design and hosting firm, a digital marketing consultancy, and a wedding planning firm. She's organized and curated multiple TEDx events and hired to assist other nonprofit organizations as a fractional executive, including The Travel Institute and The Freelance Association.

As a writer, speaker, and trainer she believes in the power of words and their ability to heal, inspire, incite, and motivate. Her greatest inspiration is her daughters, Kelsea and Cathryn, who tolerate her tendency to run away from home to play with her friends around the world for months at a time. It's said she could run a small country with just the contents of her backpack.

Alice Briggs, Creative Director

As the creative director of Indie Author Magazine, Alice Briggs utilizes her more than three decades of artistic exploration and expression, business startup adventures, and leadership skills. A serial entrepreneur, she has started several successful businesses. She brings her experience in creative direction, magazine layout and design, and graphic design in and outside of the indie author community to her role.

With a masters of science in Occupational Therapy, she has a broad skill set and uses it to assist others in achieving their desired goals. As a writer, teacher, healer, and artist, she loves to see people accomplish all they desire. She's excited to see how IAM will encourage many authors to succeed in whatever way they choose. She hopes to meet many of you in various places around the world once her passport is back in use.

Nicole Schroeder, Editor in Chief

Nicole Schroeder is a storyteller at heart. As the editor in chief of Indie Author Magazine, she brings nearly a decade of journalism and editorial experience to the publication, delighting in any opportunity to tell true stories and help others do the same. She holds a bachelor's degree from the Missouri School of Journalism and minors in English and Spanish. Her previous work includes editorial roles at local publications, and she's helped edit and produce numerous fiction and nonfiction books, including a Holocaust survivor's memoir, alongside independent publishers. Her own creative writing has been published in national literary magazines. When she's not at her writing desk, Nicole is usually in the saddle, cuddling her guinea pigs, or spending time with family. She loves any excuse to talk about Marvel movies and considers National Novel Writing Month its own holiday.

Writers

Laurel Decher

There might be no frigate like a book, but publishing can feel like a voyage on the H.M.S. Surprise. There's always a twist and there's never a moment to lose.

Laurel's mission is to help you make the most of today's opportunities. She's a strategic problem-solver, tool collector, and co-inventor of the "you never know" theory of publishing.

As an epidemiologist, she studied factors that help babies and toddlers thrive. Now she writes books for children ages nine to twelve about finding more magic in life. She's a member of the Society for Children's Book Writers and Illustrators (SCBWI), has various advanced degrees, and a tendency to smuggle vegetables into storylines.

Gill Fernley

Gill Fernley writes fiction in several genres under different pen names, but what all of them have in common is humour and romance, because she can't resist a happy ending or a good laugh. She's also a freelance content writer and has been running her own business since 2013. Before that, she was a technical author and documentation manager for an engineering company and can describe to you more than you'd ever wish to know about airflow and filtration in downflow booths. Still awake? Wow, that's a first! Anyway, that experience taught her how to explain complex things in straightforward language and she hopes it will come in handy for writing articles for IAM. Outside of writing, she's a cake decorator, expert shoe hoarder, and is fluent in English, dry humour and procrastibaking.

Kasia Lasinska

Kasia Lasinska holds an LLB in Law with European Legal Studies and an LL.M. in Advanced Studies in International Law. As a practicing attorney, Kasia worked with a top international human rights barrister and then advised clients at a large, international law firm. These inspired her to write dystopian and fantasy novels about corrupt governments and teenagers saving the world.

Kasia has lived in eight countries and speaks five languages (fluently after a glass of wine). She currently lives in London, but her daydreams are filled with beaches and palm trees.

When she's not writing, you can find Kasia scouting out the best coffee shops in town, planning her next great adventure, or petting other people's puppies.

Angie Martin

Award-winning author Angie Martin has spent over a decade mentoring and helping new and experienced authors as they prepare to send their babies into the world. She relies on her criminal justice background and knack for researching the tiniest of details to assist others when crafting their own novels. She has given countless speeches in various aspects of writing, including creating characters, self-publishing, and writing supernatural and paranormal. She also assisted in leading a popular California writers' group, which organized several book signings for local authors. In addition to having experience in film, she created the first interactive murder mystery on Clubhouse and writes and directs each episode. Angie now resides in rural Tennessee, where she continues to help authors around the world in every stage of publication while writing her own thriller and horror books, as well as branching out into new genres.

Angie was raised in a mixed home, Caucasian and Mexican, and has successfully written about other cultures throughout her career.

Merri Maywether

Merri Maywether lives with her husband in rural Montana. You can find her in the town's only coffee house listening to three generations of Montanans share their stories. Otherwise, she's in the classroom or the school library, inspiring the next generation's writers.

Jenn Mitchell

Jenn Mitchell writes Urban Fantasy and Weird West, as well as culinary cozy mysteries under the pen name, J Lee Mitchell. She writes, cooks, and gardens in the heart of South Central Pennsylvania's Amish Country. When she's not doing these things, she dreams of training llama riding ninjas.

She enjoys traveling, quilting, hoarding cookbooks, Sanntangling, and spending time with the World's most patient and loving significant other.

Susan Odev

Susan has banked over three decades of work experience in the fields of personal and organizational development, being a freelance corporate trainer and consultant alongside holding down "real" jobs for over twenty-five years. Specializing in entrepreneurial mindsets, she has written several non-fiction business books, once gaining a coveted Amazon #1 best seller tag in business and entrepreneurship, an accolade she now strives to emulate with her fiction.

Currently working on her fifth novel, under a top secret pen name, the craft and marketing aspects of being a successful indie author equally fascinate and terrify her.

A lover of history with a criminal record collection, Susan lives in a retro orange and avocado world. Once described by a colleague as being an "onion," Susan has many layers, as have ogres (according to Shrek). She would like to think this makes her cool, her teenage children just think she's embarrassing.

Ready to level up your indie author career?

Trick question. Of course you are.

*INDIE ^Author Tools

Get Your Friday Five Newsletter and find your next favorite tool here.

https://writelink.to/iat

Join the Facebook group here.

https://writelink.to/iatfb

Get documents done anywhere

Now available for your Android & iOS mobile device

Dragon® Anywhere professional-grade mobile dictation makes it easy to create documents of any length, edit, format and share them directly from your mobile device-whether visiting clients, a job site, or your local coffee shop.

- Continuous dictation and no word limits
- 99% accurate with powerful voice editing and formatting
- Access customized words and auto-text across all devices
- Share documents by email, Dropbox, Evernote and more

Select a flexible pricing plan Subscribe now ▾ *Credit Card Required. After your 7 day free trial, the monthly subscription begins at $15 per month. Cancel at anytime.

WriteLink.To/Dragon

Are you our next Featured Author?

Tell us your story!

writelink.to/featured

MERCH FOR AUTHORS

Branded merch on Etsy, Amazon, and your own site.
Learn about extended stock licenses.
Includes sample contracts.

envato elements

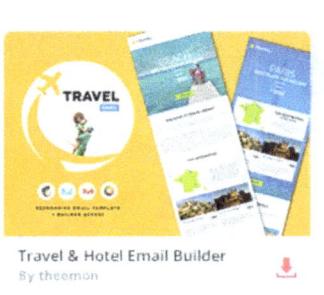

Travel & Hotel Email Builder
By theemon

Travel Email Builder
By HyperPix

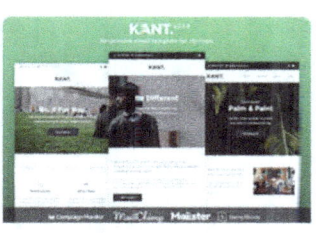

Kant - Email Template
By ThemeMountain

Olive - Fashion Email Template
By giantdesign

Metro App - Instapage Template
By Morad

ButaPest Email Template
By JeetuG

All the Email Templates you need and many other design elements, are available for a monthly subscription by subscribing to Envato Elements. The subscription costs $16.50 per month and gives you **unlimited access** to a massive and growing library of **1,500,000+** items that can be downloaded as often as you need (stock photos too)!

DOWNLOAD NOW